An Introduction:
The Brontës

and their
Poetry

Anne Crow

Published by Crowscapes

ISBN: 978-0-9562328-2-3

Printed by www.lulu.com

Contents

Poems

All unlisted photographs were taken by the author.

Illustrations

Chronology

Date	Historical events	The Brontës
1776	American Declaration of Independence	
1777		Patrick Brontë is born .
1784	Watt invents steam engine. Wesley founds Methodism.	
1785	Edmund Cartwright invents power loom.	
1789	French Revolution and Declaration of Rights of Man	
1792	Wollstonecraft: *A Vindication of the Rights of Women* published	
1793	Execution of Louis XVI Reign of Terror in France Britain and France at war	Patrick establishes school.
1798	Nelson's victory at the Battle of the Nile Rebellion in Ireland	Patrick Brontë's school in Drumballyroney is closed. Patrick, 21, becomes a tutor.
1801	Act of Union with Ireland	
1802	Peace of Amiens	Patrick is admitted to St John's College, Cambridge
1803	Renewal of war against France	
1805	Nelson's victory at Trafalgar	
1806		Patrick is awarded first class degree. He is ordained.
1807	Abolition of slave trade in British Empire	
1810		*Cottage Poems* published

1811	Prince of Wales becomes Regent Luddite riots	
1812		Patrick Brontë marries Maria Branwell.
1813		*The Rural Minstrel* published
1814	Abdication of Napoleon Stephenson's steam locomotive	Maria is born.
1815	Battle of Waterloo Corn Law passed prohibiting imports to keep price high	Elizabeth is born. Patrick is appointed curate at Thornton.
1816	Game Laws are passed.	*The Cottage in the Wood* published. Charlotte is born.
1817	Habeas Corpus Act suspended *Blackwood's Magazine* launched	Branwell is born.
1818	Habeas Corpus Act restored	Emily Jane is born.
1819	'Peterloo' Massacre at civil rights demonstration outside Manchester	Patrick is offered perpetual curacy of Haworth.
1820	Death of George III Accession of George IV	Anne is born. The family moves to Haworth in April.
1821		Mrs Brontë dies. Her sister, Elizabeth Branwell comes to nurse her and stays.
1824		Maria and Elizabeth go to Cowan Bridge School, then Charlotte and Emily. The bog bursts. *The Phenomenon* is published.
1825	Opening of Stockton and Darlington Railway	Maria and Elizabeth die. Charlotte & Emily go home.
1826		Branwell given soldiers which inspire Glasstown sagas

1831	Unsuccessful introduction of Reform Bills; widespread riots	Charlotte goes to Roehead School.
1832	Reform Act is passed, starting electoral reform process.	Patrick opens Sunday School. Charlotte returns to Haworth to teach her sisters.
1833	Controls placed on child labour by passage of Factory Act	
1834	Abolition of slavery in British Empire	
1835	Municipal Reform Act	Branwell trains as a painter. Charlotte teaches at Roe Head Emily goes as pupil; soon returns ill, then Anne goes.
1836	Chartist movement founded	C. B. sends poems to Southey.
1837	Accession of Queen Victoria	Anne ill, returns to Haworth
1838	*People's Charter* is published	Charlotte leaves Roe Head. Emily takes a teaching post. Branwell moves to Bradford.
1839	Chartist's petition is rejected by Parliament.	Branwell abandons career as portrait painter; Charlotte and Anne become governesses.
1840	First presentation of *People's Charter* to Parliament	Branwell works as a tutor, then works on railway. Anne starts work at Thorp Green
1841		CB's second job as governess Branwell promoted. *Halifax Guardian* publishes first of twelve poems by Branwell.
1842	Second Chartist petition rejected. Chartist riots near Haworth and elsewhere violently stopped by military.	Charlotte and Emily attend Pensionnat Heger in Brussels. Branwell is dismissed. Aunt Branwell dies, so the sisters return home.

1843	Robert Southey, poet laureate, dies.	Charlotte returns to Brussels, falls in love with M. Heger.
		Branwell appointed tutor at Thorp Green
1844	Royal Commission on Health in Towns	Charlotte returns home. Plans for a school at Haworth fail.
1846	Repeal of Corn Laws Famine in Ireland	Publication of *Poems* by Currer, Ellis and Acton Bell. It does not sell, so the sisters start writing novels.
1847	Ten Hours Act limits working day in textile mills for women and adolescents.	*Jane Eyre* (CB), then *Wuthering Heights* (EJB) and *Agnes Grey* (AB) published.
1848	Third Chartist petition rejected There are Chartist rallies in Haworth and riots in Bradford. Public Health Act	*The Tenant of Wildfell Hall* (AB) is published September: Branwell dies; December: Emily dies.
1849		Anne dies; *Shirley* (CB) is published
1850		Babbage's *Report to the General Board of Health* initiates improvements in Haworth.
1853		*Villette* (CB) is published.
1854	Crimean War breaks out. First Working Man's College is opened.	Charlotte marries Arthur Bell Nicholls, and she becomes pregnant.
1855		31st March, Charlotte dies.
1857		*The Professor* [Charlotte's first novel] is published.
1861		Patrick Brontë dies.

Patrick Brontë

Patrick Brontë was born on St Patrick's Day, 17th March, 1777, in a modest two-roomed thatched cottage in the parish of Drumballyroney, County Down. His father, Hugh, was a farmer and also a charismatic storyteller and poet in the oral tradition. Patrick's parents were hard-working, and gradually their circumstances improved until, by the time the last of their ten children was born, they were living in a large two-storey stone-built house.

Patrick Brontë's birthplace

Patrick, the eldest child, was allowed to remain at school longer than was usual, possibly as a pupil-teacher. He was very ambitious, and in 1793, at the age of sixteen, he opened his own school, next to the church. However, inspired by the French Revolution, the Society of United Irishmen rebelled against English rule, determined to establish social and political reform in Ireland. Patrick's younger brother joined the rebels, but he managed to avoid capture when they were defeated. Patrick was not a rebel, but the suppression of this rebellion may have been the cause of the closure of Patrick's school in 1798.

Drumballyroney Church and the school Patrick established

At the age of 21, he took up an appointment as tutor to the children of Reverend Thomas Tighe, an influential member of the landed gentry and a member of the Evangelical movement in the Church of Ireland. It is likely that his employer coached Patrick in Latin and Greek so that he could apply to university with a view to becoming ordained. Having been accepted by St John's College, Cambridge, on his employer's recommendation, Patrick sailed for England in July 1802. At 25, Patrick was a lot older than most of the other students, and he had not had their privileged upbringing. Even without his strong Irish accent, he would have been an outsider.

St John's College, Cambridge

Like the three other sizars, or scholarship students, he would have had to make a substantial contribution towards his fees and supply his own heating and candles, although his room and food were paid for. To earn money he did some private tuition, and he won cash awards and books for excellent performance in examinations. Patrick was accustomed to scrimping and saving, but he needed more money than he could earn or win. He committed himself to a career in the Church of England and was lucky to find sponsors in Henry Thornton, patron of one of the Evangelical societies, and William Wilberforce, the famous abolitionist.

Patrick was not always engrossed in his books, however. He was a tall, strong, athletic man, and, when it was feared that Napoleon was planning to invade England, he was quick to join a volunteer corps at the university. Under the command of Lord Palmerston, who would later become Prime Minister, the volunteers spent an hour every day in military drill.

Patrick graduated on 23rd April, 1806. Not only was he one of only seven students to be awarded a first class degree, but he was one of only five who had managed to gain first class results throughout his time at Cambridge. Significantly, he spent his graduation gift from the college, not on a religious tome, but on Sir Walter Scott's newly published poem, *The Lay of the Last Minstrel.*

Ordination

By the time he was applying for ordination, Patrick had standardized his surname, which had previously been spelt in various ways. Brontë is not only a more gentlemanly spelling than Brunty or Prunty, it is also the

Greek word for thunder, which seems very appropriate for his resonant sermons. However, he probably took this form of the name in imitation of his hero, Lord Nelson, whose Sicilian title was The Duke of Brontë.

Patrick had several appointments before he settled in Haworth. He served in the parish of Wethersfield, in Essex, from October 1806 until January 1809. From there he moved to Wellington in Shropshire, where he stayed less than a year.

He had always wanted to live and work in Yorkshire, which was apparently regarded by Evangelicals as a 'Promised Land' of opportunity, and Bradford was a fast-growing parish, because of the textile industry. So, when he was offered the post of curate in Dewsbury, an industrial town near Bradford, he accepted, in spite of having been also offered the attractive post of chaplain to the governor of Martinique in the West Indies.

'Cottage Poems'

Dewsbury Parish Church

It was while he was at Dewsbury that Patrick started to send his poetry off for publication. One long rambling poem, in which he expresses his thoughts about a variety of subjects, was published anonymously in 1810. He then adapted it and included it in **_Cottage Poems_**, a volume of poetry which he published the following year. In regular rhyming couplets, the opening section of **Winter Night Meditations** gives a graphic picture of the suffering of the poor in winter:

from: *Winter Night Meditations*

Rude winter's come, the sky's o'ercast,
The night is cold and loud the blast,
The mingling snow comes driving down,
Fast whitening o'er the flinty ground.
Severe their lots whose crazy sheds
Hang tottering o'er their trembling heads:
Whilst blows through walls and chinky door
The drifting snow across the floor,
Where blinking embers scarcely glow,
And rushlight only serves to show
What well may move the deepest sigh,
And force a tear from pity's eye.
You there may see a meagre pair,
Worn out with labour, grief, and care:
Whose naked babes, in hungry mood,
Complain of cold and cry for food,
Whilst tears bedew the mother's cheek,
And sighs the father's grief bespeak;
For fire or raiment, bed or board,
Their dreary shed cannot afford.

He calls for the fortunate to *'confer relief'* and bestow *'a part/ Of God's donation.'* The next section of this sermon in poetry then warns of the dangers of city life and the evils of prostitution. However, he is sympathetic when he tells the story of how a young girl was brought to a life of shame, blaming not her but the abstract concept of *'vice'*:

> *Once she was gentle, fair, and kind,*
> *To no seducing schemes inclined,*
> *Would blush to hear a smutty tale,*
> *Nor ever strolled o'er hill or dale,*
> *But lived a sweet domestic maid,*
> *To lend her aged parents aid -*
> *And oft they gazed and oft they smiled*
> *On this their loved and only child:*
> *They thought they might in her be blest,*
> *And she would see them laid at rest.*
>
> *A blithesome youth of courtly mien*
> *Oft called to see this rural queen:*
> *His oily tongue and wily art*
> *Soon gained Maria's yielding heart.*
> *The aged pair, too, liked the youth,*
> *And thought him naught but love and truth.*
> *The village feast at length is come;*
> *Maria by the youth's undone:*
> *The youth is gone - so is her fame,*
> *And with it all her sense of shame:*

And now she practises the art
Which snared her unsuspecting heart,
And vice, with a progressive sway,
More hardened makes her every day.
Averse to good and prone to ill,
And dextrous in seducing skill,
To look, as if her eyes would melt;
T' affect a love she never felt;
To half suppress the rising sigh;
Mechanically to weep and cry;
To vow eternal truth, and then
To break her vow, and vow again.
Her ways are darkness, death, and hell;
Remorse and shame and passions fell,
And short-lived joy, with endless pain,
Pursue her in a gloomy train.

The moral he draws is that Sin brings misery, but
Religion can bring consolation:

Where Sin abounds Religion dies,
And Virtue seeks her native skies;
Chaste Conscience hides for very shame,
And Honour's but an empty name.
Then, like a flood, with fearful din,
A gloomy host comes pouring in.

First Bribery, with her golden shield,
Leads smooth Corruption o'er the field;
Dissension wild, with brandished spear,
And Anarchy bring up the rear:
Whilst Care and Sorrow, Grief and Pain
Run howling o'er the bloody plain.

In another section of these **'Meditations'**, he tells a dramatic story of a shipwreck. He calls on his readers to listen in their imaginations as he uses onomatopoeia to describe the *'clanking'* of the pumps, and then the *'crashing shock'* as the fragile ship *'shivered'* against the *'solid'* rock. These two contrasting words emphasise the vulnerability of the ship, which he personifies as a delicate female who ends up in her *'wat'ry grave'*. By contrast, the elements are portrayed as sentient monsters, revelling in the battle. The wind raves *'in wild destruction'*, the waves are *'fierce'* and the tide *'hostile'*, until heavy monosyllables describe how *'down she sinks!'* and the winds are *'triumphant'*.

The fact that the description is conveyed in only two long sentences, together with the use of the present tense and rhyming couplets, speeds up the pace until the tragic ending. To increase the tension, he disrupts the rhythm with breaks in the middle of lines and exclamations, and he runs some of the lines on into the next, achieving a dramatic immediacy which grips the reader:

> *But hark! the bleak, loud whistling wind!*
> *Its crushing blast recalls to mind*
> *The dangers of the troubled deep,*
> *Where, with a fierce and thundering sweep,*
> *The winds in wild distraction rave*
> *And push along the mountain wave*
> *With dreadful swell and hideous curl!*
> *Whilst hung aloft in giddy whirl,*
> *Or drop beneath the ocean's bed,*
> *The leaky bark without a shred*
> *Of rigging sweeps through dangers dread.*
> *The flaring beacon points the way,*

And fast the pumps loud clanking play:
It 'vails not -- hark! with crashing shock
She's shivered 'gainst the solid rock,
Or by the fierce, incessant waves
Is beaten to a thousand staves;
Or bilging at her crazy side,
Admits the thundering hostile tide,
And down she sinks! - triumphant rave
The winds, and close her wat'ry grave!

This is poetry in the oral tradition, and Patrick draws no moral from this particular story. In this passage, he is more poet than pastor, harnessing the power of words to produce dramatic poetry, and his message seems peripheral. He concludes that, if we embrace Religion, *'December turns to smiling May'*, a metaphor which conveys the idealised message that, through a strong religious faith, everyone can find salvation and happiness and be protected from the storms of life.

Another poem in the collection **_Cottage Poems_** is directly addressed to the ordinary people for whom he intended these verses. In the introduction, Patrick says that he "has aimed at simplicity, plainness, and perspicuity, both in manner and style" to appeal to homely folk.

from: ***Epistle To The Labouring Poor***

All you who turn the sturdy soil,
Or ply the loom with daily toil,
And lowly on through life turmoil
    For scanty fare,
Attend, and gather richest spoil
    To soothe your care.

I write with tender, feeling heart -
Then kindly read what I impart;
'Tis freely penned, devoid of art,
    In homely style,
'Tis meant to ward off Satan's dart,
    And show his guile.

This **Epistle** lacks the dramatic power of **Winter Night Meditations.** In some of his poems we can feel the "real, indescribable pleasure" which he found in his writing, but in this one he seems to have been merely doing his job and writing a sermon in a more palatable form. He tries to convince the poor that they are lucky because they are not exposed to the temptations of the rich, and he offers them the reassurance that, if they repent their sins, they will find glory in the life after death. Patrick Brontë was surrounded by dreadful poverty, and he no doubt wanted to offer his parishioners some consolation.

Poverty

The West Riding of Yorkshire depended on the textile industry. New more efficient machinery, housed in mills, was putting traditional cottage industries out of business. Landowners wanting to rear sheep evicted their tenants, who had to seek work in towns. Famine in Ireland brought desperate people flocking into the area, prepared to take very low wages. The war with France disrupted supplies of wool and cotton and cut off important markets for finished cloth, so even those with jobs were frequently laid off or put on short time.

The government did nothing to alleviate the distress of starving people, looking after the interests of their electorate - landowners. Common land, on which people had been allowed to graze their animals, was enclosed. Corn Laws prevented the import of cheap grain. Game Laws punished poaching with seven years' transportation. Desperate to feed their families, some men tried to halt the technological advances which were putting them out of work by destroying the new machinery. They called themselves Luddites after Ned Ludd who led the first such attack in Leicestershire.

Luddites

In 1811, Patrick moved to Hartshead, where Luddites were active. On one occasion, a large force of Luddites, all from Patrick's parish, marched on Rawfolds Mill, near Hartshead, where the owner, William Cartright, had been introducing new machinery. Mr. Cartright had called in the military; the Luddite force was repelled. Two men were killed and many wounded. A later attempt to murder Cartright failed, but another local manufacturer, William Horsfall, was killed. In 1813, 17 Luddites were executed, including three for the murder of Horsfall and five for the attack on Rawfolds Mill.

Although he was sympathetic to the plight of those desperate men, Patrick knew that violence was not the answer. He uttered vehement warnings from the pulpit, strongly advising his parishioners against participating in these attacks, and he sided with the establishment in condemning them. This put him into real danger, and it was probably at this time that he formed his lifelong habit of keeping a loaded pistol by his bed. He discharged it out of the window every morning, because that was the only way of removing the bullet and making the gun safe.

In July 1812, Patrick met Maria Branwell, who had travelled from her home in Penzance to visit relatives in Yorkshire. Maria was 29, petite and elegant, well-educated and witty, with an engaging personality. Patrick was 35, a good-looking and lively red-haired Irishman, whom Maria once referred to as "my own saucy Pat". Theirs was a whirlwind romance, and it is thought that Patrick proposed on a visit to the romantic ruins of Kirkstall Abbey, on the banks of the River Aire. Before the end of the year, they were married.

Kirkstall Abbey 1804

The Rural Minstrel

In September 1813, Patrick published his next volume of verse _The Rural Minstrel:_ *A Miscellany of Descriptive Poems*. Like his previous poems, these were intended for people with little money or leisure time. One of the poems in _The Rural Minstrel_ is set in the ruins of Kirkstall Abbey, which Patrick compares with an elderly wise man watching over the *'smiling landscape'*:

from: **Kirkstall Abbey**

Hail ruined tower! That, like a learnèd sage,
With lofty brow, looks thoughtful on the night;
The sable ebony and silver white,
Thy ragged sides from age to age
With charming art inlays,
When Luna's lovely rays
Fall trembling on the night,
And round the smiling landscape throw,
And on the ruined walls below,
Their mild uncertain light.
How heavenly fair the arches ivy-crowned
Look forth on all around!

In the introduction to **_Cottage Poems_**, Patrick described poetry as "a channel, through which the warm effusions of the heart might be poured with delightful facility and with the most powerful effect". In this new volume, he included a very personal poem addressed to his beloved wife on the occasion of her thirtieth birthday:

from: ***Lines addressed to a lady on her birthday.***

Maria, let us walk and breathe the morning air
And hear the cuckoo sing, -
And every tuneful bird that woos the gentle spring.
Throughout the budding grove,
Softly coos the turtle-dove,
The primrose pale
Perfumes the gale.
The modest daisy and the violet blue,
Inviting, spread their charms for you.

How much enhanced is all this bliss to me,
Since it is shared in mutual joy with thee!
And should our vernal sky with clouds o'ercast
Be rent by whirlwinds and the sweeping blast;
Should thunders roll
From pole to pole

And shake the fearful world,
E'en then, thy sweet society would cheer the gloom
And light a ray of hope
And bear my spirits up,
And all my keener griefs, to blank oblivion hurled,
Absorbed in her illimitable womb,
Would leave the softened mind
Arrayed in solemn joy, -
Whilst thou dost love, and still art kind,
No gloomy changes can my peace destroy.

In the introduction to **_The Rural Minstrel,_** Patrick explains that, "The author has preferred writing the greater part of his little volume in the irregular metre, as it is sanctioned by the authority of some of the most eminent authors, is most congenial to his own mind, and seemed to him best calculated for poems of a descriptive nature." The irregular rhyme scheme and line lengths help his thoughts to sound spontaneous, even though they are carefully crafted. These lines are no conventional exercise in writing love poetry but a "warm effusion of the heart" that leaves readers in no doubt of the depth of his love for his wife.

For Patrick Brontë, to walk in the countryside in all its moods was to rejoice in the glory of his God who had created this beautiful world, as he explains in this extract from a more regular poem, entitled *Rural Happiness:*

The smile of spring, the fragrant summer's breeze,
The fields of autumn, and the naked trees,
Hoarse, braying, thro' winter's doubling storms;
E'en rural scenery, in all its forms,
When pure religion, rules the feeling heart –
Compose the soul, and sweetest joys impart.
With heart enraptured, oft have I surveyed
The vast and bounteous works that God has made.
The tinkling rill, the flood's astounding roar,
The river's brink, and ocean's frothy shore,
The feathered songster's notes, and winter's howl,
The sky serene, and frowning ether's scowl,
The softest sound, the hoarsest thunder's roll,
Have each their sweetest pleasures for my soul.

As roves my mind o'er nature's works abroad,
It sees, reflected, their creative God:
The insects dancing in the sunny beam,
Whose filmy wings like golden atoms gleam,
The finny tribe that glance across the lake,

The timid hare that rustles through the brake,
The squirrel blithe that frisks on yonder spray,
The wily fox that prowls about for prey,
Have each a useful lesson for my heart,
And soothe my soul, and rural sweets impart.

However, in a poem entitled **Winter,** also in **The Rural Minstrel,** his thoughts are filled with compassion for the wildlife and for the poor, who have only a flimsy shed to protect them from the weather. He begs God and his readers to relieve the suffering of these unfortunates:

from: **Winter**

In hops the redbreast, half afraid –
Ah! Lend the little stranger aid,
Throw gently o'er the floor,
With silent twitch, a fallen crumb;
And lest grimalkin*, prowling come –
Close fast the dreaded door.

Ill fares the lowly hapless shed
Where, o'er their nightly slumbers spread,

**'grimalkin'* is an old grey cat. (cf: the witches' cat in *Macbeth)*

The chilling, drifted snow
Congeals their blood and breaks their rest,
And wakes the terrors of their breast
To keenest sense of woe.

May he who clothes the lilies fair
And feeds the wandering birds of air
Relieve their great distress!
Haste ye, who lie on beds of down,
With bounteous hand their table crown
And make their sorrow less.

Loud howls the wild, unconstant blast,
Deep sullen glooms the sky o'ercast
And all the heartless scene;
Stern winter's breath locks up the flood,
Thrills through the nerves and chills the blood,
Fierce, freezing, sharp and keen.

Thornton

Patrick and Maria's first daughter, Maria, was born in April 1814, and their second, Elizabeth, in February 1815. With a growing family, Patrick must have been glad to be offered the perpetual curacy of Thornton, which more than doubled his income. They moved in May 1815 into the parsonage, a double-fronted house on Market Street.

72 and 74 Market Street, Thornton, the former parsonage

Not far away was the Church of St James, popularly known as the Bell Chapel. Patrick found the church dilapidated and gloomy. He set about having it re-roofed and the south wall rebuilt, and he also added a second-hand cupola. A new church was erected in 1872 on the opposite side of the road, and the Bell Chapel soon fell into disrepair. However, the cupola survives and is proudly placed on a plinth near the ruined chapel:

The cupola of the old Bell Chapel, with the ruins of the east window behind

It was in Thornton that Patrick wrote and published a story, *The Cottage in the Wood, or the art of becoming rich and happy*. The four poems published with it are sermons in a palatable form rather than "effusions of the heart". The reader feels that the poet is merely doing his job rather than engaged in employment which was "full of real, indescribable pleasure", as he had been when composing his **_Cottage Poems_**.

Maria's older sister, Elizabeth Branwell, had supported the family through the move to Thornton, but, when Charlotte was born, in April 1816, she was anxious to return home to Penzance. Patrick appointed Nancy Garrs, trained at the Bradford School of Industry, as nursemaid; she was only thirteen years old. Only a little more than a year later, Maria gave birth to a son, Patrick Branwell, followed by Emily the following year. With five children under the age of five, Patrick realized that Maria needed more help, and Nancy's sister, Sarah, came to look after the children while her sister became cook and assistant housekeeper.

The vicar of Bradford appointed Patrick Brontë to the perpetual curacy of Haworth in June 1819, but his appointment met with intransigent resistance from the church trustees, who resented interference in their affairs. Patrick resigned the appointment, and Samuel Redhead was appointed in his place. The congregation subjected Reverend Redhead to a sustained campaign designed to humiliate him, and he was eventually driven out.

On 17th January, 1820, the Brontës' sixth child, Anne, was born. All the children except Maria, the eldest, were baptized in the Bell Chapel, and the font can still be seen in the new Church of St James.

In February, Patrick was reappointed to the curacy of Haworth with the agreement of the church trustees. However, it was not until April that the family moved to their new home in the rectory at Haworth.

Haworth

Early in the nineteenth century, Haworth was a busy industrial town, lying on one of the main trade routes between Yorkshire and Lancashire. It is situated in the hills above Keighley and Bradford, with an ample supply of water, so it was also an ideal place to site factories. When the Brontës moved to Haworth in 1820, it already had 13 small textile mills, as well as a large number of hand-loom weavers, spinners and wool-combers working in their own homes.

The population was increasing rapidly because of the quickly expanding textile industry. The photograph of three cottages overleaf gives us some idea of the cramped conditions in which families lived. The top floor is thought to have been a workshop, running the length of the building. Each cottage was home to three families. Wool-combers, whose occupation created a large amount of heat and steam, worked and lived with their families in the poorly ventilated basements. On the first floor there were two back-to-back homes for the weavers and their families.

Former weavers' cottages in West Lane, Haworth

Living conditions were very primitive. There was no sanitation at all, no sewers and few covered drains. The liquid waste, including that from privies, ran along open channels and gutters down the streets. Solid waste, also including the refuse from privies, was collected for farm manure in walled enclosures in the back yards known as middensteads, which would sometimes overflow and create an even worse health hazard.

There were no water closets in Haworth and only 69 privies, one of which was at the Rectory. Most households shared a privy with up to 23 other families, so it is not surprising that mortality rates were among the highest in Britain. Average age at death was only 25.

An early twentieth century photograph of Haworth Main Street,

With no running water, people had to fetch water from one of the few pumps, and in summer the pumps ran so slowly that people had to start queuing in the middle of the night to get water for the morning. The Rectory was lucky enough to have its own pump in the kitchen, and, in his diary for September 1847, Patrick Brontë notes: "Had the well cleaned out. It had not been cleaned for 20 years. The water was tinged yellow by eight tin cans in a state of decomposition." If this was the state of a private well, it is horrifying to imagine the state of public ones.

Overcrowding, inadequate housing, lack of sanitation, no running water, low wages, poor standards of nutrition, ignorance and lack of effective medical treatment all contributed to the spread of disease. Tuberculosis accounted for about a quarter of all deaths. Other major killers were typhus, cholera and influenza, which were more or less endemic, but reached epidemic proportions frequently. A particular danger in Haworth was 'wool-sorter's disease', which commonly affected sheep and is spread by spores. We now know this as anthrax, which has been used in biological warfare.

Three out of ten children died before they reached their first birthday. One of the most poignant graves in Haworth cemetery marks the burial place of seven children in the same family, all of whom died before their second birthday.

To the right of the baby can be seen the name of the stonemason who so lovingly carved this ornate memorial – it was Joseph Heaton, their father.

An estimated 44,000 people have been buried in this overcrowded graveyard, which covers only nine-tenths of an acre. In some places the corpses are thought to have been buried ten deep. Drainage was inadequate, there were no trees and most of the gravestones are flat, which hampers decomposition of the corpses.

Reverend Brontë worked tirelessly to relieve the suffering of the poor, and he repeatedly petitioned the General Board of Health to improve sanitation. Eventually, in 1850, when the overcrowded graveyard was contaminating the already unhealthy water supply, the Board commissioned the Babbage Report, and, as a result of this, conditions began to improve.

Whenever the wool trade was struggling, conditions grew even worse for the poor, because they were laid off or put on short weeks. Patrick Brontë's strenuous efforts to raise public subscription for the relief of the poor failed because they were regarded as an underclass whose degradation was largely their own fault. It was frequently asserted that God had made them poor, and that He wished them to remain poor. Society regarded widows, orphans, old people and the chronically sick as 'deserving', and so they could receive help through the degrading system of the Poor House; anyone else was regarded as 'undeserving' and refused any help at all. With no unemployment benefit, no sick-pay and no pensions, people needed children to support them through illness and old age, so families were large and children usually sent out to work from the age of 5 or 6.

This led to another common cause of death or crippling injury in children. Mill-owners employed children as cheap labour, because they earned only a tenth of an adult wage. They were forced to work up to 14 hours a day for six days a week, without breaks. Tiredness and hunger frequently led to accidents with the machinery. The smallest children were employed as 'scavengers'; they had to creep under the machines while they were still in operation to gather up bits of loose cotton or wool. It was not until 1833 that a Reform Act was passed stating that children under nine were not permitted to work, and children from the ages of nine to eleven could only work for a maximum of 8 hours a day.

The Church of St Michael and All Angels was demolished in 1879 by Patrick's successor. Only the tower remains from the original church, and that was raised to add a clock.

As you can see in this photograph, the wall of the tower shows evidence of the rebuilding of the church. The building in the background of this photograph is the Parsonage.

Haworth Parsonage. The large gabled wing on the right was added in 1878,
and the trees were planted in 1864 to help disperse the corpses.

The Parsonage, now the Brontë Museum, overlooks the church and the graveyard at the front and lies at the top of Haworth's steeply cobbled Main Street. Although the building is now surrounded by car parks and houses, from the rear the Brontës would have had an uninterrupted view of the moors.

Haworth Main Street and the Black Bull Inn

Tragedy

Less than a year after they moved, Mrs. Maria Brontë was taken dangerously ill. She was suffering from cancer, and for months she endured agonizing pain. As she grew weaker, Patrick hired a nurse to look after her when his duties called him away, but he always nursed her devotedly during the long nights. When all the children succumbed to scarlet fever, poor Patrick was at risk of losing all those he loved. Mercifully, however, the children recovered, and soon Maria's older sister, Elizabeth Branwell, came back from Penzance to help.

With Elizabeth to help nurse Maria and support the family, the professional nurse was no longer required. She was asked to leave, but she went with a very bad grace. Many of the myths surrounding the Brontë family, and Patrick in particular, started when this bitter woman vented her spleen to Mrs. Gaskell, Charlotte's friend and biographer, who interviewed her. When Maria Brontë died on 15th September 1821, she left six children under the age of eight.

According to all the accounts of those who knew him well, Patrick was a kind, considerate and cheerful friend, employer and father. He took the children to visit his friends and on long walks on the moors. He spent as much time as he could with them, happily joining in their games and guiding their education. The children had a warm and stable childhood with their father, their affectionate aunt and the two young servants.

School

The children were very close in age and they enjoyed each other's company; they did not need to look elsewhere for friends. Their aunt, however, wished to return home to Penzance, and Patrick could not bring up five daughters on his own. He was also aware that, should he die, the children would be homeless, and so they needed to be equipped to earn their own living. He decided to send the girls to school, but it was impossible to find the fees for five. When a new school opened specifically for the daughters of clergymen, charging only half the usual fees, he decided to send his children there. The list of patrons was impressive, including Patrick's own former sponsor, William Wilberforce.

The school had only been open a few months when Maria and Elizabeth arrived in July 1824, followed in August by Charlotte. It was founded by Reverend Carus Wilson, a well-known evangelical preacher. This must have been a traumatic time for the girls. Not only were they leaving home for the first time, but they also had to say goodbye to their aunt and to the two servants, who were also leaving. Nancy and Sarah Garrs were much more than servants to the children; they were playmates and confidantes, frequently involved in the children's games, but not well enough educated to assume the responsibility of bringing up a clergyman's daughters.

Although Charlotte's account of Lowood in *Jane Eyre* is clearly based on her experiences at Cowan Bridge, and expresses her anger and resentment, it is enhanced by scandalous newspaper reports of other schools. The picture of the hypocritical Mr. Brocklehurst is a caricature, written through the eyes of Jane Eyre as a child. Nevertheless, the girls were unlucky to be there during its first winter. Every Sunday, for instance, the girls had to walk two miles to Reverend Carus Wilson's church, whatever the weather, and they were kept in the cold damp church between services.

The Clergy Daughters' School at Cowan Bridge

The Phenomenon

On 12th September, 1824, while the three oldest children were at school, the three youngest went out for a walk on the moors with the servants. It was a beautiful day, but soon Patrick observed the signs that a storm was approaching. When he heard a deep explosion and felt the earth move beneath his feet, he set out in search of them. There had been a huge bog-burst, like an earthquake, but, wisely, the servants had led the children to a safe place to take shelter.

Patrick wrote a sermon on the phenomenon and also published a poem for children in Sunday school. In the introduction to the poem, he writes that: "During the time of a tremendous storm of thunder, lightning, and rain, a part of the moors in my chapelry ... sunk into two wide cavities; the larger of which measured 300 yards in length, about 200 in breadth, and was 5 or 6 yards deep. From these cavities ran deep rivers, which, uniting at the distance of 100 yards, formed a vast volume of mud and water, varying from 30 to 60 yards in breadth, and from 5 to 6 in depth; uprooting trees, damaging, or altogether overthrowing, solid stone bridges, stopping mills, and occasionally overwhelming fields of corn, all along its course of 10 or 15 miles."

Danger

The children had, indeed, been in dreadful danger. The effects of the bog-burst were felt 17 miles away in Leeds. The day after, Patrick went up to Crow Hill to see how much damage had been caused. Two vast areas of moorland bog had been swept down the valleys by the massive volume of water which had been absorbed by the peat during the torrential rainfall of the days preceding the storm. Huge numbers of fish had been suffocated by the peat and mud. One solid stone bridge was swept away and others broken. Hedges and walls were flattened and houses were swamped. Several mills had their workings clogged up, and the woollen industry was brought to a standstill.

Although Patrick attributed the phenomenon to God, seeing the storm as a warning "to turn sinners from the error of their ways", he gives a detailed scientific explanation of how it happened. Natural underground reservoirs were overcharged by recent exceptionally heavy rain. He believed that the electrical discharge of lightning, combined with the "unusually great heat", produced considerable expansion, and, when a tremor was caused by the loud thunder, the combination caused "the surface of the ground to shake and rend, and open a passage for the struggling elements."

The poem, *The Phenomenon,* opens with a detailed description of a beautiful day when:

> *All was gold and deep ethereal blue,*
> *Save a red halo, whose portentous glare*
> *Or said or seemed to say to all – "beware!"*

When the storm has built up and is threatening to break, present participles come thick and fast to speed the pace and increase the anticipation; then he ominously slows the pace by separating the list of adjectives with both commas and conjunctions:

> Condensing fast, the black'ning clouds o'erspread
> The low'ring sky: the frequent lightning red,
> With quivering glance, the streaming clouds do sunder,
> And rumbles deep, and long, and loud, the thunder!

When the storm breaks he interrupts the regular rhythm by putting heavy stresses at the beginnings of lines. Because of their position, the monosyllabic adverbs 'Down' and 'Quick' dramatically convey the suddenness with which the rain fell and the lightning flashed:

> The tempest gathering from the murky west
> Rests on the peak and forms a horrid crest.
> Down pour the heavy clouds their copious streams,
> Quick shoots the lightning's fiercely vivid gleams,
> And loud and louder peals the crashing thunder;
> The mountains shake as they would rend asunder.

Like the traditional storytellers of his native Ireland, he calls on his readers to see the storm in their imaginations, employing vivid similes to compare *'the solid ground'* to an ocean driven by the four winds, and the torrent of water, mud, peat and débris to an avalanche in the Alps:

> *But, see! The solid ground, like ocean driven*
> *With mighty force by the four winds of heaven,*
> *In strange commotion rolls its earthy tide –*
> *Whilst the riven mountain from its rugged side*
> *A muddy torrent issues, dark and deep,*
> *That, foaming, thunders down the trembling steep,*
> *As, high on Alpine hills, for ages past,*
> *The falling snows, pil'd by the stiff'ning blast,*
> *Rise a huge mountain on the dazzled eye,*
> *Jut o'er their base, far curling in the sky,*
> *Till, by their weight, these mighty masses fail,*
> *And, breaking, thunder down the trembling vale,*
> *Bury whole towns in everlasting snow,*
> *And chill with horror pale the world below.*
> *So, rocks on rocks, pil'd by the foaming flood,*
> *All its vast force with trembling base withstood,*
> *Till the indignant waves, collecting fast,*
> *Form'd a dark lake, urged by the incumbent blast,*
> *And push'd at once, with wide resistless sway,*
> *The mighty mass, 'midst thund'ring sounds, away,*
> *Shook all the neighbouring hills, and thrill'd with fear*
> *The peasant's heart and stunn'd his listening ear!*

> *On whirring wings the startled moorcocks fly,*
> *The fleeing gunners pass unheeding by,*
> *The labouring peasants haste, with sturdy stride,*
> *To 'scape the danger of the coming tide;*
> *The bleating sheep, or heedless or too slow,*
> *The cattle with a loud, last dismal low,*
> *The bridges, trees and rocks and earthy mounds,*
> *With thundering crash and deepening hollow sounds,*
> *In dread confusion tumble in the waves*
> *Of that thick flood, that darkens, foams and raves,*
> *With loud resistless force and loosen'd rein,*
> *Threatening to whelm the wide adjacent plain.*

It gives the poem an added poignancy to think that the poet was not merely observing the bog-burst from the safety of a house but was actually out in it, frantically searching for his three little children and their minders. No wonder the details imprinted themselves on his memory to be recalled later when they were safely home.

> *As onward rolls the dark, resistless tide,*
> *Pale, trembling mortals flee on either side.*
> *The clanking engines and the busy mill,*
> *In thick obstruction deep immersed, stand still.*
> *Grim devastation lords it o'er the plain:*

The gardens' bloom, the mead, the yellow grain,
The green plantation and the brambly wood
Lie deeply buried in the murky flood.
The finny tribe to 'scape these horrors try
And, sunk in muddy suffocation, die.
The snowy geese that crop the grassy brim,
The motley ducks that, gabbling, featly swim
With unsuspecting joy, await the roar
Of that thick flood that, tangling, whelms them o'er.
All nature sinks and dies beneath the sway
Of those black waves that, ponderous, force their way
O'er trees and rocks and high-opposing mounds,
Breasting along with hollow, thund'ring sounds!

Patrick attributes the cessation of the storm to God's mercy. The reader can hear the change in the poetry as the onomatopoeic rumbling and crashing of the thunderous sounds are replaced by the gentle *'trickling'* and *'tinkling music'* of the rivulets:

But, as the fiercest passion soonest dies,
And lightest fuel first in ashes lies,
So this vast flood, that foam'd with loudest roar,
Was, self-exhausted, soonest heard no more;
For, long ere night was clad in sable vest,

It sank within its banks and went to rest;
Whilst many a muddy stream went trickling still
With tinkling music down the neighbouring hill,
And many a rivulet pursued its way,
With wid'ning surface, till another day.

The poem seems to come to an end when he explains the phenomenon as a warning of when *'God's hot ire'* will sink the earth and heavens *'in liquid fire'*. However, possibly because he was writing for children, he finishes on a more optimistic vision of *'the great Judge'* coming to collect the pious and take them to the heaven of heavens.

The moors behind the parsonage

Further Tragedy

In November, Patrick took Emily to join her sisters at Cowan Bridge School, and it seems that the older girls had no complaints at this time. However, as winter took hold, the girls suffered in the harsh weather because of the Spartan conditions. Many of the girls became ill during the school's first year and were withdrawn or sent home. In February 1825, when the school informed Patrick of Maria's illness, he went immediately to collect her, but it was too late. Eleven weeks after he took her home, on 6th May, 1825, she died of tuberculosis.

While he was nursing his eldest daughter, he was not told that Elizabeth was also very ill. There was an outbreak of typhus at the school, and they probably assumed she was suffering from this. However, when the other girls were sent to the seaside at the doctor's recommendation, Elizabeth was sent home by public transport, accompanied by only a servant.

The day after her unexpected arrival, Patrick lost no time in fetching Charlotte and Emily. Elizabeth lingered only until 15th June. This double tragedy affected the four remaining children deeply. The two older girls had been the leaders in all their games, and, to some extent, they had taken their mother's place.

Some years later, Branwell wrote a poem using a narrator called Harriet, who is mourning the death of her older sister, Caroline. Surely he must have drawn on his own painful memories as he wrote these lines. When lifted to see her sister in the coffin, Harriet admits that,

> 'To this moment, I can feel
> The voiceless gasp – the sickening chill –
> With which I hid my whitened face'.

The funeral is described in such poignant detail that it sounds like a memory:

> 'They came – they pressed the coffin lid
> Above my Caroline,
> And then, I felt, for ever hid
> My sister's face from mine!

There was one moment's wildered start –
One pang remembered well –
When first from my unhardened heart
The tears of anguish fell:
That swell of thought which seems to fill
The bursting heart, the gushing eye,
*While fades all **present,** good or ill.*
All else seems blank – the mourning march
Before the shades of things gone by,
The proud parade of woe,
The passage 'neath the churchyard arch,
The crowd that met the show.
My place or thoughts amid the train
I strive to recollect, in vain –
I could not think or see:
I cared not whither I was borne:
And only felt that death had torn
My Caroline from me.'

(from: ***Calm and clear the day declining***)

In the light of these two tragedies, Aunt Branwell
decided to stay to teach the girls. Gradually the family
rose above their loss and established a routine of lessons
in the morning and recreation in the afternoon.

The Brontë Bridge, one of the family's favourite places, which can be
reached after a walk of about two miles from the Parsonage.

Childhood: *'a land of love and light'*

It would be a mistake to think that the young Brontës were bookish children. They also had plenty of toys which they played with at length. When Branwell was twelve, his father gave him some toy soldiers; each child seized one and named him. They settled these 'Young Men' in the imaginary land of the Ashantees, on Africa's Gold Coast, and started writing the Glasstown sagas.

The children acted out their plays in the garden or on the moors, where they could shoot their enemies with cannon and dam streams to wash them away. The cellars in the Parsonage became dungeons for the incarceration of political prisoners. The siblings even invented an ancient language for their characters which was written down phonetically in their stories.

From these early plays sprung epic stories of the adventures of the leaders of the kingdoms of Angria and Gondal. At first, the children worked together on the

Glasstown sagas, but later Emily and Anne broke away and created their own kingdom of Gondal, an island in the South Pacific. Branwell and Charlotte turned to writing about Angria, a new kingdom established in the African wilderness surrounding Glasstown. The passionate stories they made up involved struggles for power and the deepest human emotions: love and hate, betrayal and revenge. At times of particular emotional intensity in the stories, they would often write a poem.

The characters in these imaginary kingdoms became mouthpieces for the siblings, and they were able to give voice to deep emotions that are usually kept private. A good example of this is Branwell's poem, an extract from which is quoted on pages 62-63. Charlotte's rousing battle hymn for the Angrians, supposedly written by Arthur Wellesley, Duke of Zamorna, is written in a contrasting mood of excitement and pride. The detailed description of the *'Patrician Pirate'*, Alexander Percy, Duke of Northangerland, suggests the influence of Lord Byron and is surely the forerunner to Mr. Rochester:

from: *A National Ode for the Angrians*

... the sullen flag of Percy swells most proudly to the breeze
As haughtily the folds unfurl as if they swept the seas!

Patrician Pirate! On each side his blighting glance is flung:
The silent scorn that curls his lip can never know a tongue!

Upon his melancholy brow a melancholy shade,
Like snow-wreaths on Aornu's slope, eternally is laid,

But the son of that tremendous sire amid the throng appears, -
His second self unpetrified by the chill lapse of years:

A form of noblest energy, most sternly beautiful;
A scimitar whose tempered edge no time can ever dull;

A sword unflush'd, a quenchless flame, a fixed and radiant star;
A noble steed caparisoned which snuffs the fight afar!

The glory of his youthful brow, the light of his blue eye,
Will flash upon the battle's verge like arrows of the sky.

With such a host, with such a train, what hand can stop our path?
Who can withstand the torrent's strength when it shall roll in wrath?

Lift, lift the scarlet banner up! Fling all its folds abroad,

And let its blood-red lustre fall on Afric's blasted sod:

For gore shall run where it has been, and blighted bones shall lie
Wherever the sun standard swelled against the stormy sky.

And when our battle-trumpets sound, and when our bugles sing,
The vulture from its distant rock shall spread its glancing wing;

And the gaunt wolf at that signal cry shall gallop to the feast:
A table in the wilderness we'll spread for bird and beast.

We'll sheath not the avenging sword till earth and sea and skies
Through all God's mighty universe shout back, 'Arise! Arise!'

Till Angria reigns Lord Paramount wherever human tongue
The 'Slaves' Lament', the 'Emperor's Hymn', in woe or bliss hath sung!

The children would write the poems, plays and stories down in tiny books made from scraps of paper, using quills to imitate print in tiny hand-writing. These were supposed to be an appropriate size for the toys, but this technique had the added advantage that adults could not read them. These imaginary worlds were by no means a simple retreat from reality, but a source of endless fun, which they still enjoyed when they were adults.

A stream on Haworth Moor

The siblings did not, however, live wholly in their imaginations, although they were protected from the town's squalor. They were well aware of what was happening in the world at large, particularly in the fields of politics and literature, and they incorporated real people and events into their stories. Haworth was no cultural desert; it had its own orchestra and lectures were held at the Foresters' Hall, as well as in the neighbouring town of Keighley.

The Brontës had access to the circulating libraries at Keighley and possibly the magnificent library at Ponden Hall, home of the Heaton family. They could also use Patrick's library, including his own published works, which must have helped to form their ambitions to be poets. They read widely, including the poetry of Sir Walter Scott, Milton, Shakespeare, Wordsworth, Shelley, Southey and even Lord Byron, whose poetry was generally thought unsuitable for ladies.

They would also regularly read a wide variety of newspapers and magazines. One of these, in particular, *Blackwood's Magazine,* a miscellany of satire and comment on contemporary politics and literature, was a strong formative influence, providing characters and settings for many of their games. Branwell even launched his own tiny magazine in direct imitation of it, and, when he grew tired of the project, Charlotte took it over. Branwell's lifelong ambition was to become a regular contributor to *Blackwood's Magazine.* It is surprising, considering their early interest in politics, that the poetry of all the siblings is usually introspective.

Although their formal education was partial and fragmented, the Brontës came from a household where all kinds of artistic pursuits were encouraged. Patrick Brontë not only provided a role model as a published writer, he also gave his children a thirst for education and the freedom, as far as he could afford, to find it wherever they could. They tried their hands at everything, shared everything, inspired each other and explored human feelings in a way that would not have been possible without siblings who were kindred spirits.

One of the favourite books in Patrick's library was Thomas Bewick's *History of British Birds*. As well as woodcuts of birds in their natural surroundings, this book features tiny vignettes telling a vast range of fascinating stories, from the amusing to the macabre, from the domestic to the supernatural. As an adult, Charlotte wrote a eulogy to Bewick:

from: **Lines on Bewick**

Our childhood's days return again in thought,
  We wander in a land of love and light,
And mingled memories, joy – and sorrow – fraught,
  Gush on our hearts with overwhelming might.

Sweet flowers seem gleaming 'mid the tangled grass
  Sparkling with spray-drops from the rushing rill,
And, as these fleeting visions fade and pass,
  Perchance some pensive tears our eyes may fill.

These soon are wiped away, again we turn
  With fresh delight to the enchanted page
Where pictured thoughts that breathe and speak and burn
  Still please alike our youth and riper age.

There rises some lone rock all wet with surge
　　And dashing billows glimmering in the light
Of a wan moon, whose silent rays emerge
　　From clouds that veil their lustre, cold and bright.

And there, 'mongst reeds upon a river's side,
　　A wild bird sits, and brooding o'er her nest
Still guards the priceless gems, her joy and pride,
　　Now ripening 'neath her hope-enlivened breast.

We turn the page: before the expectant eye
　　A traveller stands lone on some desert heath;
The glorious sun is passing from the sky
　　While fall his farewell rays on all beneath;

O'er the far hills a purple veil seems flung
    Dim herald of the coming shades of night;
E'en now Diana's lamp aloft is hung,
    Drinking the full radiance from the fount of light.

Oh, when the solemn wind of midnight sighs,
    Where will the lonely traveller lay his head?
Beneath the tester of the star-bright skies
    On the wild moor he'll find a dreary bed.

Now we behold a marble Naiad placed
    Beside a fountain on her sculptured throne,
Her bending form with simplest beauty graced,
    Her white robes gathered in a snowy zone.

She from a polished vase pours forth a stream
    Of sparkling water to the waves below
Which roll in light and music, while the gleam
    Of sunshine flings through shade a golden glow.

A hundred fairer scenes these leaves reveal;
  But there are tongues that injure while they praise:
I cannot speak the rapture that I feel
  When on the work of such a mind I gaze.

Then farewell, Bewick, genius' favoured son,
  Death's sleep is on thee, all thy woes are past;
From earth departed, life and labour done,
  Eternal peace and rest are thine at last.

These woodcuts were an ideal size for illustrating their stories. They not only fed the children's vivid imaginations, but all of them practised drawing by copying the tiny illustrations. Several of their copies can be seen in the Brontë Parsonage Museum, including Charlotte's copy of this cormorant on a stormy shore:

Another artist who inspired the Brontës was John Martin, a favourite of their father who had several of his dramatic engravings hanging on the wall of the Parsonage. Martin depicted awe-inspiring scenes, often set in magnificent cities with fantastic architecture like the buildings the siblings imagined for their private worlds. His huge Biblical canvases are as melodramatic as the stories the Brontës wrote in the Gondal and Angria epics. His paintings are as imaginative, passionate and elemental as the novels later written by the three sisters.

The children all had drawing and music lessons, and the family expected Branwell to have a distinguished career as an artist. When he decided to become a professional portrait painter, he had lessons to prepare him to enter the Royal Academy.

'Sweet dreams of home'

In 1830, Patrick fell seriously ill, and this brought home to the family the fact that, if he were to die, the children would have no home and no income. Charlotte, now fourteen, was sent away to Roe Head School in Mirfield, to equip her to earn her own living. Here she made two lifelong friends, Ellen Nussey and Mary Taylor. When she returned at the age of sixteen, she was old enough to supervise the education of her sisters as well as to teach in the newly built National Church Sunday School, situated by the Parsonage, overlooking the graveyard. As they grew up, the Brontës all taught at the school.

Now that the four of them were together again, the siblings spent much of their time engrossed in their fictional Glasstown sagas. However, in 1835, the family was separated once more when Charlotte, now nineteen, went to teach at Roe Head School, and Emily, now seventeen, accompanied her as a pupil. After this, they were rarely together. All of them write wistfully about home and their happy childhood when they are away.

Charlotte

When Charlotte was teaching at Roe Head, she wrote a long poem in which she looks back poignantly to the imaginary worlds she shared with her siblings:

from: *Retrospection*

We wove a web in childhood,
A web of sunny air;
We dug a spring in infancy
Of water pure and fair;

We sowed in youth a mustard seed,
We cut an almond rod;

We are now grown up to riper age -
Are they withered in the sod?

Are they blighted, failed and faded,
Are they mouldered back to clay?
For life is darkly shaded;
And its joys fleet fast away.

Faded! the web is still of air,
But how its folds are spread,
And from its tints of crimson clear
How deep a glow is shed.
The light of an Italian sky,
Where clouds of sunset lingering lie,
Is not more ruby-red.

Charlotte evokes four natural images to suggest the imaginative inspiration the four children shared: a web, spring water, a mustard seed and an almond rod. The web caught their dreams and allowed them to bring their fantasies to life. It was once pure and simple, like *'sunny air'*, but, as she extends the image in the fourth stanza, we realize that, now she is an adult, the childhood fantasy is even more important. No longer does it only reflect light, as they imitated their favourite writers, now it generates a rich crimson light from its own nature.

The Brontë waterfall

Each image is developed to its extreme to reflect the way their childish attempts at writing have become confident, powerful and individual voices. The pure spring water, another image for their childhood inspiration, has become an ocean. The mustard seed, an allusion to the parable in which Jesus compared the Kingdom of Heaven to a grain of mustard, has grown into a mighty tree. The fourth metaphor, the almond rod, is a reference to the Biblical story of Aaron's rod which budded, bloomed and fruited. Her use of biblical images suggests that she thought their inspiration was holy. The tiny seed of fantasy planted when they were children has become a strong and enduring world of myth which the four siblings can still call on for solace when far from home.

In December 1836, hoping to leave teaching and earn her living from writing, Charlotte wrote to the poet laureate, Robert Southey, sending some of her poems for his consideration. His reply was disheartening: "The day dreams in which you habitually indulge are likely to produce a distempered state of mind …Literature cannot be the business of a woman's life, and it ought not to be." Hopelessly believing that she was destined for a lifetime in teaching, she wrote the following poem:

from: *The Teacher's Monologue*

... Now, as I watch that distant hill,
  So faint, so blue, so far removed,
Sweet dreams of home my heart may fill,
  That home where I am known and loved:
It lies beyond; yon azure brow
  Parts me from all Earth holds for me;
And, morn and eve, my yearnings flow
  Thitherward tending, changelessly.
My happiest hours, ay! All the time,
  I love to keep in memory,
Lapsed among moors, ere life's first prime
  Decayed to dark anxiety.

... To toil, to think, to long, to grieve, -
  Is such my future fate?
The morn was dreary, must the eve
  Be also desolate?
Well, such a life at least makes Death
  A welcome, wished-for friend;
Then aid me Reason, Patience, Faith
  To suffer to the end!

Charlotte made two unsuccessful attempts to be a governess, the only other career open to an educated woman. The educated offspring of the impoverished gentry and clergy were in great demand as tutors and governesses by those entrepreneurial members of the working class who had become wealthy due to the Industrial Revolution and who wished to raise their social status. She decided that, if she had to be a teacher, she could at least aim for independence. The sisters hatched a plan to open a school, which would remove the necessity of servitude to people with inferior minds. Aunt Branwell offered them a loan, and Charlotte and Emily set off to the Pensionnat Heger in Brussels to improve their language skills.

Branwell

Branwell did not enrol in the Royal Academy, but there were plans for him to make a study tour of the continent. Hoping to make useful contacts, he gained admittance to the Freemasons, who used to meet at The Black Bull, a public house which is adjacent to the church:

The plans for a continental tour came to nothing, but he painted some portraits in Haworth and worked as a portrait painter in Bradford for a while.

Branwell joined the boxing club which met at the inn, and he loved to meet travellers to learn the news. He was such a regular visitor that he even had his own special chair which can be found on the stairs of the inn.

In January 1840, Branwell took up a position as a tutor in Cumbria. Still hoping to carve out a literary career, he sent samples of his original poems and translations to, among others, the poet, Hartley Coleridge, son of Samuel Taylor Coleridge. Coleridge alone replied, inviting Branwell to visit him in the Lake District.

This translation of Horace's ode on the transience of life and the universal truth that death comes to all people equally, disregarding wealth and power, is a good example of how Branwell translated poems freely from Latin and, in doing so, made them his own:

To Sestius

Rough winter melts beneath the breeze of spring,
*   Nor shun refitted ships the silenced sea,*
Nor man nor beasts to folds or firesides cling,
*   Nor hoar frosts whiten over field and tree;*
But rising moons each balmy evening see
Fair Venus with her Nymphs and Graces join
*   In merry dances tripping o'er the lea;*
While Vulcan makes his roaring furnace shine,
And bids his Cyclops arms in sinewy strength combine.

Now let us, cheerful, crown our heads with flowers,
  Spring's first fruits, offered to the newborn year,
And sacrifice beneath the budding bowers,
  A lamb, or kid, as Faunus may prefer:
  But – pallid Death, an equal visitor,
Knocks at the poor man's hut, the monarch's tower;
  And the few years we have to linger here
Forbid vain dreams of happiness and power
Beyond what man can crowd into life's fleeting hour.

Soon shall the night that knows no morning come
  And the dim shades that haunt the eternal shore
And Pluto's shadowy kingdom of the tomb,
  Where Thee the well thrown dice may never more
  Make monarch, while thy friends the wine cup pour;
Where never thou mayest woo fair Lycidas,
  Whose loveliness our ardent youth adore;
Whose faultless limbs all other forms surpass,
And, lost amid whose beams, unseen all others pass.

At midsummer, Branwell was dismissed from his post as
tutor; the reason can only be guessed at. He polished up
more of his translations and sent them to Coleridge,
who, sadly, never replied, although a draft letter has

been found in which he praises Branwell's versification and the power and energy of the poems.

Branwell soon managed to secure a job as assistant clerk-in-charge at Sowerby Bridge on the newly constructed railway line between Leeds and Manchester. By April 1841, he had been promoted to the position of clerk-in-charge at Luddenden Foot, and he was still optimistic of finding fame and fortune as a writer, encouraged by having poems published in the *Halifax Guardian*. Branwell wrote a lot of poetry during his time at Luddenden Foot, including *'The desolate earth'*. This long poem opens with a description of the dreary December weather:

from: *'The desolate earth'*
The desolate earth, the wintry sky,
The ceaseless rain-showers driving by –
The farewell of the year –
Though drear the sight, and sad the sound,
While bitter winds are wailing round,
Nor hopes depress, nor thoughts confound,
Nor waken sigh or tear.

For, as it moans, December's wind
Brings many varied thoughts to mind
　　Upon its storm-drenched wing,
Of words, not said 'mid sunshine gay,
Of deeds, not done in summer's day,
Yet which, when joy has passed away,
　　Will strength to sorrow bring.

For, when the leaves are glittering bright,
And green hills lie in noonday night,
　　The present only lives;
But, when within my chimnies roar
The chidings of the stormy shower,
The feeble present loses power,
　　The mighty past survives.

I cannot think – as roses blow,
And streams sound gently in their flow,
　　And clouds shine bright above –
Of aught but childhood's happiness,
Of joys unshadowed by distress
Or voices tuned the ear to bless
　　Or faces made to love.

The poet reflects that, when the weather is fine, he thinks only of 'Childhood's happiness/ Of joys unshadowed by *distress'*. He goes on, however, to assert that, in the violent storms of December, *'The Soul gains strength'*, and he has the *'will and power to rise/ Above the present day'*:

> *But, when these winter evenings fall*
> *Like dying nature's funeral pall,*
> > *The Soul gains strength to say*
> *That – not aghast at stormy skies –*
> *That – not bowed down by miseries -*
> *Its thoughts have will and power to rise*
> > *Above the present day.*

> *So winds amid yon leafless ash,*
> *And yon swollen streamlet's angry dash,*
> > *And yon wet howling sky,*
> *Recall the victories of mind*
> *O'er bitter heavens and stormy wind*
> *And all the wars of humankind –*
> > *Man's mightiest victory!*

He is inspired to celebrate the achievements of men such as Galileo, Dr Johnson and Robert Burns, who overcame adversity to achieve immortality. The reader is left to conclude that Branwell believes he also will triumph and become famous. Sadly, he lost his job because he was held responsible for some irregularities in the accounts, although he was not suspected of theft. His optimism was clearly crushed by this experience because, soon after his return from Luddenden, the following sonnet was published in *The Halifax Guardian.* It is tempting to think that it is autobiographical, expressing Branwell's own doubts in religion, in spite of the best efforts of his father and his aunt.

On Peaceful Death and Painful Life

Why dost thou sorrow for the happy dead?
  For, if their life be lost, their toils are o'er,
  And woe and want can trouble them no more;
Nor ever slept they in an earthly bed
So sound as now they sleep, while dreamless laid
  In the dark chambers of the unknown shore
  Where Night and Silence guard each sealed door.
So turn from such as these thy drooping head,
  And mourn the **Dead-Alive** *- whose spirit flies -*
Whose life departs before his death has come;
  Who knows no Heaven beneath Life's gloomy skies,
Who sees no Hope to brighten up that gloom,
  'Tis **He** *who feels the worm that never dies,*
The **real** *death and darkness of the tomb.*

In the first half, the poet questions why we mourn for the dead, because their troubles are over and they sleep soundly. The second half claims that the people who need our pity are those who are **'Dead Alive'** - those who have lost the will to live, but have no consoling faith in an after-life to give them hope.

Later that year, 1842, Aunt Branwell died, and Branwell told a friend, "I have now lost the guide and director of all the happy days connected with my childhood". Anne recommended him to her employers as a tutor, and he started work at Thorp Green in January. He found it very difficult to adjust to being a tutor again, after being in charge at Luddenden Station.

Soon after his arrival, he wrote a nostalgic poem regretting the passing of the happy times he had known as a child. He personifies Memory as an agent which brings happiness when his spirits are low, and speculates that Memory will renew his breath when he is dying:

Thorp Green

I sit, this evening, far away
From all I used to know,
And nought reminds my soul today
Of happy long ago.

Unwelcome cares, unthought-of fears,
Around my room arise;
I seek for suns of former years,
But clouds o'ercast my skies.

Yes – Memory, wherefore does thy voice
Bring old times back to view,
As thou wouldst bid me not rejoice
In thoughts and prospects new?

I'll thank thee, Memory, in the hour
When troubled thoughts are mine –
For thou, like suns in April's shower,
On shadowy scenes wilt shine.

I'll thank thee when approaching death
Would quench life's feeble ember,
For thou wouldst e'en renew my breath
With thy sweet word 'Remember'!

Emily

When Emily was a pupil at Roe Head School, she was
desperately unhappy. After a couple of months the lack
of freedom made her so ill that she had to return home. It
was three years before she left again to take a post as a
teacher at Law Hill. This time she managed to endure it
for six months before her health broke down. While there
she found some solace in writing poetry.

Her spirits were temporarily lifted one stormy
November day when she recalled an ancient song about
Spring. The changed word order of the first line gives
the effect of the poem opening with the roar of a storm,
but then the first line of a song awakens her memory of
spring, and the rhythm changes to one more jubilant.
The song's second line, *"It was morning, the bright sun was
beaming"*, reminds her of when she used to wake at dawn
and go out onto the moors with her brother and sisters:

'Loud without the wind was roaring'

Loud without the wind was roaring
Through the waned autumnal sky;

Drenching wet, the cold rain pouring
    Spoke of stormy winters nigh.

All too like that dreary eve
Sighed within repining grief -
Sighed at first - but sighed not long -
Sweet - How softly sweet it came!
Wild words of an ancient song -
Undefined, without a name:

'It was spring, for the skylark was singing:'
Those words they awakened a spell;
They unlocked a deep fountain whose springing
Nor Absence nor Distance can quell.

In the gloom of a cloudy November,
They uttered the music of May;
They kindled the perishing ember
Into fervour that could not decay.

Awaken on all my dear moorlands,
The wind in its glory and pride!
O call me from valleys and highlands
To walk by the hill-river's side!

It is swelled with the first snowy weather;
The rocks they are icy and hoar
And darker waves round the long heather
And the fern-leaves are sunny no more.

There are no yellow stars on the mountain,
The blue-bells have long died away
From the brink of the moss-bedded fountain,
From the side of the wintery brae –

But lovelier than cornfields all waving
In emerald and scarlet and gold,
Are the heights where the north-wind is raving,
And the glens where I wandered of old -

'It was morning, the bright sun was beaming.'
How sweetly that brought back to me
The time when nor labour nor dreaming
Broke the sleep of the happy and free.

But blithely we rose as the dusk heaven
Was melting to amber and blue,
And swift were the wings to our feet given
While we traversed the meadows of dew.

For the moors, for the moors where the short grass
Like velvet beneath us should lie!
For the moors, for the moors where each high pass
Rose sunny against the clear sky!

For the moors, where the linnet was trilling
Its song on the old granite stone –
Where the lark, the wild sky-lark, was filling
Every breast with delight like its own.

What language can utter the feeling
That rose when, in exile afar,
On the brow of a lonely hill kneeling
I saw the brown heath growing there.

It is impossible to read these lines aloud without feeling her elation. The uplifting rhythm and the run-on lines combine with the frequent repetition to carry the reader aloft to share in her delight and exultation. Her love for the moors shines through the sensual detail as she remembers the feel of the grass like velvet, and the *'trilling'* song of the linnet.

Soon, however, she is reminded by the scattered and stunted brown heather of her *'exile'* – a word which poignantly conveys her sadness. 'Sadness', however, is too weak a word to describe how Emily's spirit *'burned to be free'.*

> *It was scattered and stunted, and told me*
> *That soon even that would be gone:*
> *It whispered, "The grim walls enfold me,*
> *I have bloomed in my last summer's sun."*

> *But not the loved music whose waking*
> *Makes the soul of the Swiss die away*
> *Has a spell more adored and heart-breaking*
> *Than in its half-blighted bells lay.*

The spirit that bent 'neath its power,
How it longed, how it burned to be free!
If I could have wept in that hour,
Those tears had been heaven to me.

Well, well, the sad minutes are moving
Though loaded with trouble and pain;
And sometime the loved and the loving
Shall meet on the mountains again.

Anne

When Emily returned from Roe Head, Anne took her place. It was the first time that she had left home, and she was very unhappy, but she felt that she owed it to the family to gain the education needed to earn her own living. Two years later, however, she was brought low by a severe attack of gastric fever, which seems to have been made worse because she was suffering from a crisis of faith. Physically she recovered quickly once she returned home, but her religious depression lingered. Nevertheless, even when she doubted that she would be one of the saved, she did not lose her faith in God.

Some three months later, she found herself a position as a governess. She was dismissed at the end of the year, but, undaunted, she soon acquired a new position at Thorp Green. She appeared calm, but the poetry she wrote then reveals her sadness. In **Past Days**, she contrasts past happiness with her present life where there is no *'kindred heart'*. Childhood is remembered as a time of harmonious kinship and enjoyment, when the four children were as one. She compares the friendship between the four siblings with a river, *'constant and strong'*. While most of the poem is speaking of her happy memories, the first and last verses highlight the words which express the misery of the present. At Thorp Green she rises reluctantly every morning to *'joyless labour'*.

Past Days

*'Tis strange to think there **was** a time*
  When mirth was not an empty name,
When laughter really cheered the heart,
  And frequent smiles unbidden came,
And tears of grief would only flow
In sympathy for others' woe;

When speech expressed the inward thought,
   And heart to kindred heart was bare,
And Summer days were far too short
   For all the pleasures crowded there,
And silence, solitude, and rest -
Now welcome to the weary breast -

Were all unprized, uncourted then,
   And all the joy one spirit showed,
The other deeply felt again;
   And friendship like a river flowed,
Constant and strong its silent course,
For nought withstood its gentle force:

When night, the holy time of peace,
   Was dreaded as the parting hour;
When speech and mirth at once must cease,
   And Silence must resume her power;
Though ever free from pains and woes,
She only brought us calm repose.

And when the blessèd dawn again
   Brought daylight to the blushing skies,
We woke, and not **reluctant** then
   To joyless **labour** did we rise,

But full of hope, and glad and gay,
We welcomed the returning day.

Anne had inherited a sense of duty which made her grit
her teeth and persevere. She endured five years at Thorp
Green, mourning for the wildness of the moors:

Lines Written at Thorp Green

That summer sun, whose genial glow
Now cheers my drooping spirit so,
  Must cold and distant be
And only light our northern clime
With feeble ray, before the time
  I long so much to see.

And this soft, whispering breeze, that now
So gently cools my fevered brow,
  This too, alas! must turn
To a wild blast, whose icy dart
Pierces and chills me to the heart,
  Before I cease to mourn.

And these bright flowers I love so well,
Verbena, rose and sweet bluebell,
  Must droop and die away;

Those thick, green leaves, with all their shade
And rustling music, they must fade,
 And every one decay.

But if the sunny summer time
And woods and meadows in their prime
 Are sweet to them that roam,
Far sweeter is the winter bare
With long dark nights and landscapes drear
 To them that are at Home!

In another poem, Anne describes appreciatively the lovely scenery around Thorp Green and the beautifully tended garden. She, however, longs for *'the barren hills'* and the neglected garden at Haworth Parsonage:

Home

 How brightly glistening in the sun
 The woodland ivy plays!
 While yonder beeches from their barks
 Reflect his silver rays.

That sun surveys a lovely scene
 From softly smiling skies,
And wildly through unnumbered trees

The wind of winter sighs;

Now loud it thunders o'er my head
And now in distance dies,
But give me back my barren hills
Where colder breezes rise,

Where scarce the scattered, stunted trees
Can yield an answering swell,
But where a wilderness of heath
Returns the sound as well.

Penistone Hill, behind the Parsonage

For yonder garden, fair and wide,
With groves of evergreen,
Long winding walks, and borders trim,
And velvet lawns between –

Restore me to that little spot,
With grey walls compassed round,
Where knotted grass neglected lies,
And weeds usurp the ground.

Though all around this mansion high
Invites the foot to roam,
And though its halls are fair within –
Oh, give me back my HOME!

The Parsonage garden photographed from the churchyard

'the joy of liberty'

Like their father, the four siblings loved the Romantic poets. Romantic thinkers were inspired by the revolution in America, with its declaration of human rights, by the French revolutionary cry of 'Liberty, Equality, Fraternity', and by the abolition of the slave trade. They argued not just for freedom for themselves, but also for reforms in society, asserting that every individual has the same rights. Patrick was a member of the establishment and strongly opposed to revolution, but he worked tirelessly for reform. His poetry is inspired by his social concern as well as by his intense love of nature.

Nature was all important to the Romantics, and they prized emotion and imagination above reason and logic. The poetry of the four Brontë siblings is more introspective than their father's. They are concerned with their own feelings and their need for freedom. Charlotte and Branwell were both inspired to write about their hopeless passions for someone who was already married, presumably believing that love should conquer everything.

Emily, however, sought freedom for her soul. According to the following short poem, she was happiest when she was alone, and she could immerse herself in a visionary experience, feeling her soul released from her body:

'I'm happiest when most away'

I'm happiest when most away
I can bear my soul from its home of clay
On a windy night when the moon is bright
And the eye can wander through worlds of light –

When I am not and none beside –
Nor earth nor sea nor cloudless sky –
But only spirit wandering wide
Through infinite immensity.

It could be that Emily was thinking of the soul being released in death. In one of her Gondal poems, she describes a mystic experience when a prisoner tells her visitor, Julian, that *'a messenger of Hope'* comes to her every night and offers her *'eternal liberty'* in exchange for a *'short life'*.

From: *Julian M. and A.G. Rochelle*

'Yet tell them, Julian, all, I am not doomed to wear
Year after year in gloom and desolate despair;
A messenger of Hope comes every night to me
And offers, for short life, eternal liberty.

'He comes with western winds, with evening's wandering airs,
With that clear dusk of heaven that brings the thickest stars;
Winds take a pensive tone and stars a tender fire,
And visions rise and change which kill me with desire –

'Desire for nothing known in my maturer years
When joy grew mad with awe at counting future tears;
When, if my spirit's sky was full of flashes warm,
I knew not whence they came, from sun or thunderstorm;

'But first a hush of peace, a soundless calm descends;
The struggle of distress and fierce impatience ends;
Mute music soothes my breast – unuttered harmony
That I could never dream till earth was lost to me.

In order to suggest the peace that comes when her spirit is released from the confines of life on earth into the heavens, Emily uses the apparently contradictory descriptions of *'mute music'* and the *'unuttered harmony'* of the imagination, which is more sublime than any earthly music. However, just at the moment when her soul is about to dare *'the final bound'*, consciousness returns and she feels the chains once more. Paradoxically, only death can bring true freedom, but after death she will not be able to appreciate her liberty. Meanwhile, she can bear the anguish of returning to life after a visionary experience because, the more it tortures her, the earlier it will bring fulfilment:

> *'Then dawns the Invisible, the Unseen its truth reveals;*
> *My outward sense is gone, my inward essence feels –*
> *Its wings are almost free; its home, its harbour, found;*
> *Measuring the gulf, it stoops and dares the final bound!*
>
> *'Oh, dreadful is the check – intense the agony,*
> *When the ear begins to hear and the eye begins to see;*
> *When the pulse begins to throb, the brain to think again,*
> *The soul to feel the flesh and the flesh to feel the chain!*
>
> *'Yet I would lose no sting, would wish no torture less;*
> *The more that anguish racks, the earlier it will bless;*
> *And robed in fires of Hell, or bright with heavenly shine,*

If it but herald Death, the vision is divine.'

Anne also wrote of setting her spirit free, but, unlike Emily, she thought that she should do this through duty and religion. She wrote the following poem during the Christmas holidays of 1841 as she struggled with her desire to stay at home and not to return to Thorp Green. She was strongly aware of her own weaknesses and feared that she was too sinful to be admitted to Heaven.

Despondency

I have gone backward in the work,
The labour has not sped,
Drowsy and dark my spirit lies,
Heavy and dull as lead.

How can I rouse my sinking soul
From such a lethargy?
How can I break these iron chains
And set my spirit free?

There have been times when I have mourned
In anguish o'er the past,
And raised my suppliant hands on high,

While tears fell thick and fast,

And prayed to have my sins forgiven
  With such a fervent zeal,
An earnest grief, a strong desire,
  As now I cannot feel!

And vowed to trample on my sins,
  And called on Heaven to aid
My spirit in her firm resolves
  And hear the vows I made.

And I have felt so full of love,
  So strong in spirit then,
As if my heart would never cool
  Or wander back again.

And yet, alas! how many times
  My feet have gone astray,
How oft have I forgot my God,
  How greatly fallen away!

My sins increase, my love grows cold,
  And Hope within me dies,
And Faith itself is wavering now;

Oh, how shall I arise!

I cannot weep, but I can pray,
　Then let me not despair;
Lord Jesus, save me lest I die,
　And hear a wretch's prayer!

Captive birds

It is interesting to compare the different ways in which the two sisters react to the sight of a captive bird. Both identify with it, but Emily feels that the bird would prefer to be dead, and she too would rather be *'Eternally, entirely Free'* in death than kept *'in cold captivity':*

The Caged Bird

And like myself alone, wholly lone,
It sees the day's long sunshine glow;
And like myself it makes its moan
In unexhausted woe.

Give we the hills our equal prayer;
Earth's breezy hills and heaven's blue sea;
We ask for nothing further here
But our own hearts, the joy of liberty.

Ah! could my hand unlock its chain,
How gladly would I watch it soar
And ne'er regret and ne'er complain
To see its shining eyes no more.

But let me think that, if to-day
It pines in cold captivity,
To-morrow both shall soar away
Eternally, entirely Free.

Distressed by the bird's loss of liberty, Emily knew that, for both her and the bird, the only release would be in death. By contrast, Anne feels that the bird would be happy if only it had a companion. She seems to accept the inevitability of her loss of freedom as a governess, but finds it difficult to endure the loneliness of the life. She seems to believe that, if she had a *'faithful dear companion'*, she could be happy:

The Captive Dove

Poor restless dove, I pity thee;
  And when I hear thy plaintive moan,
I mourn for thy captivity,
  And in thy woes forget mine own.

To see thee stand prepared to fly,
  And flap those useless wings of thine,
And gaze into the distant sky,
  Would melt a harder heart than mine.

In vain - in vain! Thou canst not rise:
  Thy prison roof confines thee there;
Its slender wires delude thine eyes,
  And quench thy longings with despair.

Oh, thou wert made to wander free
  In sunny mead and shady grove,
And, far beyond the rolling sea,
  In distant climes, at will to rove!

Yet, hadst thou but one gentle mate
  Thy little drooping heart to cheer,
And share with thee thy captive state,
  Thou couldst be happy even there.

Yes, even there, if, listening by,
  One faithful dear companion stood,
While gazing on her full bright eye,
  Thou mightst forget thy native wood.

> But thou, poor solitary dove,
> Must make, unheard, thy joyless moan;
> The heart, that Nature formed to love,
> Must pine, neglected, and alone.

The wind

Both sisters write of spiritual joy inspired by nature. Two wonderful examples are these poems which celebrate the freedom of the wind on the moors. Anne uses an infectiously rapturous rhythm to convey her exultation. She quickens the pace with frequent present participles, alliteration and run-on lines to echo the gusting of the wind. For Anne, Nature has a personality and changing moods which are revealed in her use of the pathetic fallacy, imbuing natural phenomena with human emotions. The earth and seas are aroused to *'rapture'*; the dead leaves dance *'merrily,'* and the waves are *'proud'*.

Lines Composed in a Wood on a Windy Day

> My soul is awakened, my spirit is soaring
> And carried aloft on the wings of the breeze;
> For above and around me the wild wind is roaring,
> Arousing to rapture the earth and the seas.

The long withered grass in the sunshine is glancing
The bare trees are tossing their branches on high;
The dead leaves beneath them are merrily dancing,
The white clouds are scudding across the blue sky

I wish I could see how the ocean is lashing
The foam of its billows to whirlwinds of spray;
I wish I could see how its proud waves are dashing,
And hear the wild roar of their thunder to-day!

Emily chooses a similarly insistent rhythm for her jubilant description of storms and floods on the moors. This poem was written in 1836, but may have been influenced by her memories of the bog-burst when the floods left *'a desolate desert behind'*:

'High waving heather'

High waving heather, 'neath stormy blasts bending,
Midnight and moonlight and bright shining stars;
Darkness and glory rejoicingly blending,
Earth rising to heaven and heaven descending,
Man's spirit away from its drear dongeon sending,
Bursting the fetters and breaking the bars.

All down the mountain-sides, wild forest lending
One mighty voice to the life-giving wind;
Rivers their banks in the jubilee rending,
Fast through the valleys a reckless course wending,
Wider and deeper their waters extending,
Leaving a desolate desert behind.

Shining and lowering and swelling and dying,
Changing for ever from midnight to noon;
Roaring like thunder, like soft music sighing,
Shadows on shadows advancing and flying,
Lightning-bright flashes the deep gloom defying,
Coming as swiftly and fading as soon.

The natural world rejoices in the storm, and *'Man's spirit'* is released from the *'drear dongeon'* of everyday life. As in Anne's poem, Emily plays with patterns of consonant sounds and uses lots of present participles to force the pace onwards as the poet revels in the excitement of the storm. She exults in the freedom of the *'life-giving wind'* and the rivers as they break their banks in this *'jubilee'*, a carefully chosen word which describes an occasion of joyful celebration.

When the real *'world without'* grew too hopeless for her, Emily retreated into her imagination, where she could find the liberty she craved. In this poem, she personifies her imagination as her true friend who, together with herself and *'Liberty'*, has *'sovereignty'* over her inner world. Reason and Truth may trample on *'The flowers of Fancy'*, her escapist dreams, but her Imagination, her creative powers, will always bring solace and hope:

To Imagination

When weary with the long day's care,
And earthly change from pain to pain,
And lost, and ready to despair,
Thy kind voice calls me back again -
Oh, my true friend! I am not lone
While thou canst speak with such a tone!

So hopeless is the world without,
The world within I doubly prize;
Thy world, where guile and hate and doubt
And cold suspicion never rise;
Where thou and I and Liberty,
Have undisputed sovereignty.

What matters it that all around
Danger and guilt and darkness lie,
If but within our bosom's bound
We hold a bright, untroubled sky,
Warm with ten thousand mingled rays
Of suns that know no winter days?

Reason, indeed, may oft complain
For Nature's sad reality,
And tell the suffering heart how vain
Its cherished dreams must always be,
And Truth may rudely trample down
The flowers of Fancy, newly-blown:

But thou art ever there, to bring
The hovering vision back, and breathe
New glories o'er the blighted spring
And call a lovelier life from death.
And whisper with a voice divine
Of real worlds as bright as thine.

I trust not to thy phantom bliss,
Yet, still, in evening's quiet hour
With never-failing thankfulness,
I welcome thee, benignant Power;

Sure solacer of human cares
And sweeter hope, when hope despairs.

Whereas Anne forced herself to leave home and earn her own living, Emily made only one brief attempt. It appears that she may sometimes have felt that she should not spend so much time seeking liberty through the world of her imagination. In the following poem, she admits that she is *'Often rebuked'*, possibly by her own conscience rather than the family:

Stanzas

Often rebuked, yet always back returning
To those first feelings that were born with me,
And leaving busy chase of wealth and learning
For idle dreams of things which cannot be:

Today, I will not seek the shadowy region:
Its unsustaining vastness waxes drear;
And visions rising, legion after legion,
Bring the unreal world too strangely near.

I'll walk, but not in old heroic traces,
And not in paths of high morality,

And not among the half-distinguished faces,
  The clouded forms of long-past history.

I'll walk where my own nature would be leading:
  It vexes me to choose another guide:
Where the gray flocks in ferny glens are feeding;
  Where the wild wind blows on the mountain side.

What have those lonely mountains worth revealing?
  More glory, and more grief than I can tell:
The earth that wakes one human heart to feeling
  Can centre both the worlds of Heaven and Hell.

She decides to leave behind the world of Gondal, which is *'unsustaining'* and has come *'too strangely near'*, and not to seek refuge in books. She plans to walk on the moors, and she celebrates the natural world where she can find everything that the imagination can provide. In the mountains she can find *'more glory'* and *'more grief'* than she can imagine, and, for her, it is in the natural world that she finds her religion, both *'Heaven and Hell'*.

Hope and Despair

Following their ambition to open their own school at Haworth, Charlotte and Emily made rapid progress at the Pensionnat Heger in Brussels. M. Heger, the husband of the directrice and an eminent teacher at the Athénée Royale, recognized their talent and encouraged their creativity. The sisters returned home in November 1842, when their aunt died, but, whereas Emily thankfully took her aunt's place as housekeeper, Charlotte returned to Brussels in January as a teacher. Gradually the respect she had for M. Heger developed into hero-worship and a grand passion such as one of her characters in the Angrian saga might have suffered from.

Charlotte

M. Heger had held her in high regard as a pupil, and he continued to encourage her studies when she was teaching, but he did not encourage her attachment to him. Suffering greatly from the pangs of unrequited love, she returned home at the end of the year. She wrote him passionate letters, but he had the good sense to respond only with polite interest in her. Her despair inspired several poems, including this one in which she describes her letters to him as miserably humble:

'He saw my heart's woe, discovered my soul's anguish'

He saw my heart's woe, discovered my soul's anguish
   How in fever, in thirst, in atrophy it pined;
Knew he could heal, yet looked and let it languish, -
   To its moans spirit-deaf, to its pangs spirit-blind.

But once a year he heard a whisper low and dreary
   Appealing for aid, entreating some reply;
Only when sick, soul-worn, and torture-weary,
   Breathed I that prayer, heaved I that sigh.

He was mute as is the grave, he stood stirless as a tower;
   At last I looked up, and saw I prayed to stone:
I asked help of that which to help had no power,
   I sought love where love was utterly unknown.

Idolater I kneeled to an idol cut in rock!
   I might have slashed my flesh and drawn my heart's best blood:
The Granite God had felt no tenderness, no shock;
   My Baal had not seen nor heard nor understood.

In dark remorse I rose; I rose in darker shame;
  Self-condemned I withdrew to an exile from my kind;
A solitude I sought where mortal never came,
  Hoping in its wilds forgetfulness to find.

Now, Heaven, heal the wound which I still deeply feel;
  Thy glorious hosts look not in scorn on our poor race;
Thy King eternal doth no iron judgement deal
  On suffering worms who seek forgiveness, comfort, grace.

He gave our hearts to love: He will not Love despise,
  E'en if the gift be lost, as mine was long ago;
He will forgive the fault, will bid the offender rise,
  Wash out with dews of bliss the fiery brand of woe,

And give a sheltered place beneath the unsullied throne,
  Whence the soul redeemed may mark Time's fleeting
                              course round earth,
And know its trials overpast, its sufferings gone,
  And feel the peril past of Death's immortal birth.

In the poem, she portrays M. Heger as her idol, *'The Granite God'*, and accepts that her suffering is deserved because she strayed from God. Ashamed and *'self-*

condemned' she withdrew to *'an exile from my kind'*, eventually finding relief in the certainty of God's forgiveness. In fact, however, her self-loathing was overcome through the cathartic effect of writing about her passion in her novels and, of course, her poetry.

Charlotte did not attempt to find another job, but she did try unsuccessfully to secure some pupils for the proposed school. The school scheme was abandoned, but, in the autumn of 1845, Charlotte found a volume of Emily's private poems. This discovery jolted her out of the despair she had been suffering from since her return from Brussels. Impressed by their quality, she conceived the plan of the three sisters sending a selection of their poems away to be published under the masculine pseudonyms of Currer, Ellis and Acton Bell. Emily was angry at this invasion of her privacy, but, eventually, Charlotte managed to persuade her to collaborate. Many of the poems had been written for Gondal and Angria, so they needed careful revision to stand alone.

Published poets

Charlotte found a publisher who would print the volume at the sisters' expense, and the first copies arrived at the Parsonage on 7th May 1846. The reviews were favourable, but in the year following publication, only two copies were sold. The sisters decided to turn their attention from poetry to novels, believing that the novel was the literary form most likely to sell.

The sisters had kept their venture into publishing secret from Branwell, who must have been devastated when he found out. Just four days after the books arrived, Anne wrote a poem in which she bemoans the loss of harmony in the family home. It seems likely that *'Domestic Peace'* was disrupted by Branwell who resented having been excluded from the publishing venture:

Domestic Peace

Why should such gloomy silence reign,
And why is all the house so drear,
When neither danger, sickness, pain,
Nor death, nor want, has entered here?

We are as many as we were
   That other night, when all were gay
And full of hope, and free from care;
   Yet is there something gone away.

The moon without, as pure and calm,
   Is shining as that night she shone;
But now, to us, she brings no balm,
   For something from our hearts is gone.

Something whose absence leaves a void —
   A cheerless want in every heart;
Each feels the bliss of all destroyed,
   And mourns the change — but each apart.

The fire is burning in the grate
   As redly as it used to burn;
But still the hearth is desolate,
   Till mirth, and love, with **peace** return.

'Twas **peace** that flowed from heart to heart,
   With looks and smiles that spoke of heaven,
And gave us language to impart
   The blissful thoughts itself had given.

Domestic peace - best joy of earth!
When shall we all thy value learn?
White angel, to our sorrowing hearth,
Return, - oh, graciously return!

Branwell

In July 1845, Branwell was dismissed from his post at Thorp Green. It appears that, like Charlotte, he had conceived a grand passion for the spouse of his employer, Mrs Robinson, the mother of the boy he was tutoring. He returned home but was inconsolable. To take his mind off his despair, he went on holiday with a friend, John Brown, and they took a pleasure cruise along the North Wales coastline.

Branwell not only sketched Penmaenmawr mountain, but he also wrote a poem in grand heroic couplets. He identified with the mountain because it is beset by storms and drenched by mists, like the tears he was shedding for his *'angel's gentle breast and sorrowing face'*. The fort on its summit, once strong, is now destroyed, like his own youthful vigour and determination. He begs for a breast of steel so that, like the mountain, he can remain unmoved by the storms of life:

Penmaenmawr

Penmaenmawr

These winds, these clouds, this chill November storm
Bring back again thy tempest-beaten form
To eyes that look upon yon dreary sky
As late they looked on thy sublimity;
When I, more troubled than thy restless sea,
Found, in its waves, companionship with thee.
'Mid mists thou frownedst over Arvon's shore,
'Mid tears I watched thee over ocean's roar,
And thy blue front, by thousand storms laid bare,
Claimed kindred with a heart worn down by care.

No smile had'st thou, o'er smiling fields aspiring,
And none had I, from smiling fields retiring.
Blackness, 'mid sunlight, tinged thy slaty brow;
I, 'mid sweet music, looked as dark as thou.
Old Scotland's song, o'er murmuring surges borne,
Of 'times departed – never to return',
Was echoed back in mournful tones from thee,
And found an echo, quite as sad, in me.
Waves, clouds and shadows moved in restless change,
Around, above and on thy rocky range,
But seldom saw that sovereign front of thine
Changes more quick than those which passed o'er mine.
And as wild winds and human hands, at length,
Have turned to scattered stones the mighty strength
Of that old fort, whose belt of boulders grey
Roman or Saxon legions held at bay;
So had, methought, the young, unshaken nerve –
That, when WILL wished, no doubt could cause to swerve,
That on its vigour ever placed reliance,
That to its sorrows sometimes bade defiance –
Now left my spirit, like thyself, old hill,
With head defenceless against human ill;
And, as thou long hast looked upon the wave
That takes, but gives not, like a churchyard grave,
I, like life's course, through ether's weary range,

Never know rest from ceaseless strife and change.

But, PENMAENMAWR! a better fate was thine,
Through all its shades, than that which darkened mine:
No quick thoughts thrilled through thy gigantic mass
Of woe for what might be, or is, or was;
When Britain rested on thy giant power;
Thou hadst no feeling for the verdant slope
That leant on thee as man's heart leans on hope;
The pastures, chequered o'er with cot and tree,
Though thou wert guardian, got no smile from thee;
Old ocean's wrath their charm might overwhelm,
But thou could'st still keep thy unshaken realm –
While I felt flashes of an inward feeling
As fierce as those thy craggy form revealing
In nights of blinding gleams, when deafening roar
Hurls back thy echo to old Mona's shore.
I knew a flower whose leaves were meant to bloom
Till Death should snatch it to adorn the tomb,
Now, blanching 'neath the blight of hopeless grief
With never blooming and yet living leaf;
A flower on which my mind would wish to shine,
If but one beam could break from mind like mine:
I had an ear which could on accents dwell
That might as well say 'perish!' as 'farewell!'

An eye which saw, far off, a tender form
Beaten, unsheltered, by affliction's storm:
An arm - a lip - that trembled to embrace
My angel's gentle breast and sorrowing face,
A mind that clung to Ouse's fertile side
While tossing - objectless - on Menai's tide!
Oh, Soul! That draw'st yon mighty hill and me
Into communion of vague unity,
Tell me, can I obtain the stony brow
That fronts the storm, as much unbroken now
As when it once upheld the fortress proud,
Now gone, like its own morning cap of cloud?
Its breast is stone. Can I have one of steel,
To endure – inflict – defend – yet never feel?
It stood as firm when haughty Edward's word
Gave hill and dale to England's fire and sword,
As when white sails and steam-smoke tracked the sea,
And all the world breathed peace, but waves and me.

Let me, like it, arise o'er mortal care,
All woes sustain, yet never know despair;
Unshrinking face the grief I now deplore,
And stand, through storm and shine, like moveless
   PENMAENMAWR!

When Mr. Robinson died on 26th May, 1846, Branwell was euphoric, convinced that the woman he loved would turn to him. However, she knew what society's opinion of a marriage with a penniless tutor seventeen years younger than her would be, and her feelings for him were not strong enough to face this. Branwell never recovered from the shattering of his hopes. The most sociable of the siblings, he had always enjoyed a drink, but now he turned to alcohol and, probably, opium to deaden the pain and drown the despair.

Perhaps, if the sisters had included him in their publication, this would have given him encouragement and support to rise above his despair, but he was hardly in a state to collaborate on the project. He could not find refuge in writing because his efforts simply reinforced his unhappiness. The last poem of his to appear in print, in June 1847, was one he had written for the Angrian saga some ten years previously. He revised it before sending it to the *Halifax Guardian:*

'The End of All'

In that unpitying winter's night,
  When my own wife – my Mary – died,
I, by my fire's declining light,
  Sat comfortless, and silent sighed.
  While burst unchecked grief's bitter tide,
As I methought, when she was gone,
  Not hours, but years like this must bide,
And wake, and weep, and watch alone ...

I could not bear the thoughts which rose
  *Of what **had** been and what **must** be,*
But still the dark night would disclose
  Its sorrow-pictured prophecy:
  Still saw I – miserable me,
Long – long nights else – in lonely gloom,
  With time-bleached locks and trembling knee,
Walk aidless – hopeless – to my tomb.

In the poem, the Earl of Northangerland, hero of his Angrian saga and Branwell's pseudonym, mourns the death of his wife and sees nothing to look forward to but death. Branwell, who had been thought the most talented of the Brontës and had looked forward to a glittering career, now felt for himself the despair he had described so vividly from his imagination. He gave in to his despair, refusing to find another job, blackmailing his father and stealing in order to obtain money for drink and opium to drown his sorrows.

He was often drunk, and his behaviour was unpredictable, even violent, so Patrick took him into his own bedroom to watch over him. He began to suffer from fainting fits and delirium tremens. As his constitution was weakened by alcohol, he was vulnerable to bouts of influenza which masked the fact that he was suffering from tuberculosis. On 24th September, 1848, after three years of agony for himself and his family, he finally died at the age of thirty-one.

Francis Grundy, a friend from his time at the railway at Luddenden Foot, wrote a succinct summary of Branwell's personality in *Pictures of the Past:* "Poor, brilliant, gay, moody, moping, wildly excitable, miserable Brontë! No history records your many struggles after the good, your wit, brilliance, attractiveness, eagerness for all excitement – all the qualities which made you such 'good company', and dragged you down to an untimely grave."

Novelists

While they were worrying about Branwell, the sisters still managed to write their first novels, which they sent off to publishers in the summer of 1847. Emily's *Wuthering Heights* and Anne's *Agnes Grey* were accepted for publication at the authors' expense, although the publishers did not release them immediately. *The Professor*, however, was rejected, although one publisher sent an encouraging reply. Undaunted, Charlotte embarked on *Jane Eyre* which was an immediate success, and so the publishers of Emily's and Anne's novels brought them out in December. Anne's *Tenant of Wildfell Hall* was released in the summer of the following year, a couple of months before Branwell's death. The novels were all published anonymously, under their pseudonyms.

Emily

After Branwell's funeral, Emily was suffering from a persistent cold and cough, but she refused to see a doctor. No one realised that tuberculosis was setting in. As we have seen, she regarded death as a release from the confines of the world, and she did not fear it.

In the following poem, Emily proudly asserts that her soul is no feeble coward. She offers a pantheistic vision that God is a life force which can be found in all creation, even in her own breast:

'No Coward Soul Is Mine'

No coward soul is mine
No trembler in the world's storm-troubled sphere
I see Heaven's glories shine
And Faith shines equal arming me from Fear

O God within my breast
Almighty, ever-present Deity
Life, that in me has rest,
As I Undying Life, have power in Thee!

Vain are the thousand creeds
That move men's hearts, unutterably vain,
Worthless as withered weeds
Or idlest froth amid the boundless main

To waken doubt in one
Holding so fast by thy infinity
So surely anchored on
The steadfast rock of Immortality

With wide-embracing love
Thy spirit animates eternal years
Pervades and broods above,
Changes, sustains, dissolves, creates and rears.

Though Earth and moon were gone,
And suns and universes ceased to be,
And thou were left alone,
Every Existence would exist in Thee

There is not room for Death,
Nor atom that his might could render void
Since thou art Being and Breath,
And what thou art may never be destroyed.

The poet sees *'heaven's glories shine'*, and her faith means that she has no fear of death. Her *'ever-present Deity'* is Life itself, and she carries the life-force within her. She is contemptuous of all the various sects and *'creeds that move men's hearts'*; they merely encourage doubt. Emily believed that the spirit of *'Undying Life'* pervades all of creation. Even if objects such as the Earth and the Moon were gone, Life still exists, and it exists in every human being. Death is not the end because the life-force can never be destroyed. Emily died on 19th December, 1848, a victim of the tuberculosis that had taken her brother less than three months earlier and her two sisters in 1825.

Anne

By January 1849, it was clear that Anne was suffering from the same disease. Knowing how much it had hurt the family when Emily refused treatment, she stoically submitted to all the remedies offered. Patrick and Charlotte thought her patient and calm, but the poem she wrote the day after her illness was diagnosed reveals her despair:

Last Lines

A dreadful darkness closes in
   On my bewildered mind;
O let me suffer and not sin,
   Be tortured yet resigned.

Through all this world of blinding mist
   Still let me look to Thee,
And give me courage to resist
   The Tempter till he flee.

Weary I am, O give me strength
   And leave me not to faint;
Say Thou wilt comfort me at length
   And pity my complaint.

I've begged to serve Thee heart and soul,
   To sacrifice to Thee
No niggard portion, but the whole
   Of my identity.

I hoped amid the brave and strong
   My portioned task might lie,
To toil amid the labouring throng

With purpose keen and high.

But Thou hast fixed another part,
And Thou hast fixed it well;
I said so with my breaking heart
When first the anguish fell.

O Thou hast taken my delight
And hope of life away,
And bid me watch the painful night
And wait the weary day.

The hope and the delight were Thine;
I bless Thee for their loan;
I gave Thee while I deemed them mine
Too little thanks, I own.

She knew only too well what suffering was in store for her. This poem shows that what particularly distressed her was the ending of her hopes and ambitions. Despairing, she felt that God had taken away her chance to fulfil herself, and blamed herself for not giving Him enough thanks for the loan of *'the hope and the delight'*. Three weeks later she added some verses which show that she was trying to find something positive in her suffering. She says that she will gain the Christian virtue of fortitude from the pain, and hope and holiness from her distress.

> *Shall I with joy Thy blessings share*
> *   And not endure their loss,*
> *Or hope the martyr's Crown to wear*
> *   And cast away the Cross?*
>
> *These weary hours will not be lost,*
> *   These days of passive misery,*
> *These nights of darkness anguish-tost,*
> *   If I can fix my heart on Thee.*
>
> *The wretch that weak and weary lies,*
> *   Crushed with sorrow, worn with pain,*
> *Still to Heaven may lift his eyes*
> *   And strive and labour not in vain;*
>
> *That inward strife against the sins*
> *   That ever wait on suffering,*
> *To strike wherever first begins*
> *   Each ill that would corruption bring,*

That secret labour to sustain
  With humble patience every blow,
To gather fortitude from pain
  And hope and holiness from woe.

Thus let me serve Thee from my heart
  Whate'er be my written fate,
Whether thus early to depart
  Or yet a while to wait.

If Thou shouldst bring me back to life
  More humbled I should be;
More wise, more strengthened for the strife,
  More apt to lean on Thee.

Should death be standing at the gate,
  Thus should I keep my vow;
But hard whate'er my future fate
  So let me serve Thee now.

On 28th May 1849, Anne died at Scarborough, where she had gone hoping for a sea-cure. As we learned in her **Lines Composed in a Wood on a Windy Day,** she loved the sea, and that is where she wished to be buried, saving her father the distress of having to conduct the funeral of yet another of his much loved children.

Charlotte alone

Charlotte had stopped writing poetry in favour of novels, but she did attempt to find some solace in writing poems on the deaths of her two sisters:

On the Death of Anne Brontë

There's little joy in life for me,
And little terror in the grave;
I've lived the parting hour to see
Of one I would have died to save.

Calmly to watch the failing breath,
Wishing each sigh might be the last;
Longing to see the shade of death
O'er those belovèd features cast.

The cloud, the stillness that must part
The darling of my life from me;
And then to thank God from my heart,
To thank Him well and fervently;

Although I knew that we had lost
The hope and glory of our life;
And now, benighted, tempest-tossed,
Must bear alone the weary strife.

Charlotte was left to care for her elderly father alone. Eventually she found the love she craved, and she married Arthur Bell Nicholls, her father's curate, in 1854. She rejected him at first, as she had three earlier suitors, but his love was strong, and he finally won her round, in spite of her father's objections. Sadly, their happiness did not last long, as Charlotte died from complications in pregnancy just nine months later.

Patrick Brontë continued to work in Haworth, supported by his son-in-law, until he died in 1861, aged 84. He had served his parishioners in Haworth faithfully for forty-one years. So many people came to his funeral that the church was too small and several hundred mourners paid their last respects in the churchyard.

Bibliography

Barker, J. (1994) *The Brontës*, Weidenfeld and Nicolson

Barker, J. (ed) (1985) *The Brontës: Selected Poems*, Everyman

Davies, S. (ed) (1976) *The Brontë Sisters: Selected Poems*,
Carcanet Press

Horsfall Turner, J (ed) (1898) *Brontëana: Rev. Patrick
Brontë, A.B., His Collected Works and Life*, Bingley

Norris, P. (ed) (1997) *The Brontës: Selected Poems*, Everyman

Charlotte Brontë